THE LEADERSHIP STRIDE

Gilbert Chestnut

THE LEADERSHIP
STRIDE

PERSPECTIVE • PROCESS • POTENTIAL

PALMETTO
P U B L I S H I N G
Charleston, SC
www.PalmettoPublishing.com

First Edition

Paperbac ISBN: 979-8-8229-3951-6
eBook ISBN: 979-8-8229-4355-1

Contents

FOREWORD XI

PREFACE. XV

INTRODUCTION. XIX

CHAPTER ONE: LEADERSHIP CREDIBILITY 1

CHAPTER TWO: LEADERSHIP RIZZ 8

CHAPTER THREE: LEADERSHIP SASS 14

CHAPTER FOUR: LEADERSHIP OPTICS. 19

CHAPTER FIVE: LEADERSHIP MIND. 23

CHAPTER SIX: LUCID LEADERSHIP 28

CHAPTER SEVEN: LEADERSHIP CULTURE AGENT 33

CHAPTER EIGHT: LEADERSHIP TRUE 40

SUMMARY 47

AFTERWORD 49

Dedication

I dedicate this book in memory of my oldest grandson, Jonathan Oshea Starks. He will be loved and remembered forever! I speak of Jon in Chapter two, Leadership RIZZ.

I would like to thank my wife Elaine S. Chestnut of over 45 years for her support and patience as I went through the process of writing my first book. My five children, Kisha, Candice, Sharday, Ayliss and Gilbert Jr., and my 14 grandchildren provided inspiration as well. I thank God for my pastor for over three decades, the late Bishop Alfred L. Nicholson who I speak of in Chapter One. What a profound impact he's had on my life! The encouragement I've received from my only brother, Harold Chestnut, and my only sister Natley McKinnon and other family members was so needed. I am grateful for the inspiration provided by my cousin, Reverend Joann Pearson Collins without her realizing that she was. I would be remiss if I did not take this opportunity to thank my current pastor, Superintendent J. Kyle Nicholson, and my entire Gates of Faith Ministries, COGIC church family for their unwavering support. Most of all I am grateful to God for speaking to me, guiding me, and strengthening me all along the way. Without His grace and mercy, I would yet be lost.

WHAT'S BEING SAID ABOUT THIS BOOK

The Leadership Stride is a must read. The book is an exceptional resource for anyone looking to improve their leadership skills and become a more effective leader in the workplace or in any organization. It is packed with easy-to-implement ideas and strategies for creating positive change. I particularly enjoyed Mr. Chestnut's focus on servant leadership, which is so important in today's world. His toolbox leadership summaries are concise and impactful. The Leadership Stride is a game-changer for anyone looking to enhance their leadership skills. Highly recommended!

....

Larry D. Wyche

President/CEO Wyche
Leadership & Federal Contracting Consulting

Lieutenant General
US Army, Retired

Foreword

Today, the word leadership is often applied erroneously. Many consider a leader to be someone who speaks first or speaks the loudest to ensure their voice is heard over the voices of others. Many perceive leadership to be demonstrated when a boss or manager engages in the process of providing direction in self- serving projects or initiatives capitalizing on the efforts of others while garnering individual leadership accolades for themselves. The performance of the team is unrecognized, and the potential of the team's members is untapped and remains unrealized.

The impact of the misunderstanding of true leadership versus manufactured leadership has proven to be detrimental in many instances. True leadership is about the people you serve. Manufactured leadership is about the manipulation of people for personal benefit. True leadership is about taking responsibility and being accountable when others won't. Manufactured leadership is finger pointing and blaming others while uplifting oneself. As *The Leadership Stride* points out, True leadership starts with a vision and embodies respect for others and is fueled by empowering people. Manufactured leadership begins with self-interest and transactions (what you can do for me) and is fueled by exercising authority over others in a manner that demoralizes and defeats the team dynamic.

I cannot stress the importance of reading the *Leadership Stride*. The author, Gilbert Chestnut, is a unique and influential leader who I met early in my career. Gilbert demonstrated true leadership that was visionary, consistent, and full of servitude. I observed and learned what it means to be a leader that people respect, and through his teaching, I have been blessed to ascend and achieve so many career goals. I saw the elements of the *Leadership Stride* in practice every day.

I recall a specific situation where we worked at the same transportation and logistics operations center. At that time, I was a young energetic manager with significant responsibility, and I reported to Gilbert, who was the general manager. During one of our daily morning team meetings, which are usually positive and full of enthusiasm, I provided an update on the previous day's performance where the operation underachieved from my perspective. I spoke firmly to staff about the expectations for the day and stated the need for us to be better. My tone was cold, curt and condescending. When I concluded my remarks, I gently (at least I thought it was gently) tossed my notepad that I was using for my talking points onto my desk and sat down. Instantly, I could feel the office atmosphere shift. My perception is that I laid down the hammer and people now know how to proceed with improving performance for that day.

Shortly after the meeting concluded, Gilbert called me into his office. I'm thinking that I showed true leadership by "telling it like it is" and I would get kudos for demonstrating strong leadership. Gilbert noticed something different.

Instead of what I thought was demonstrating positive leadership by demanding excellence, he saw my series of actions to be deflating to staff, punctuated by the toss of my notepad onto my desk, which he observed as having the same effect of banging my fist on a table. It came across as if I was not willing to take responsibility for the team's performance and *blaming* my team for not executing, instead of *coaching* my team to improve. And he was right.

The team performed worse that day. However, Gilbert's leadership guidance pointed out, step-by- step of how my thoughts, tone, and tactics were not optimal and provided counsel of how to demonstrate true leadership through positive staff interactions. I later apologized for my behavior to my team; I spoke life and positivity into the staff, assured them that I had confidence in them and knew that we would improve if we just focused on a few steps more intently.

This different approach resulted in a different outcome, and the team excelled from that day forward. A few months later I was promoted.

Without Gilbert's correction, I would have adopted poor leadership traits and who is to say how many would've suffered as a result? I have realized since that moment the importance and the lingering impact that leadership has on those we lead and those around us. Leadership is a lifestyle, a way of thinking, speech, and action. In other words, it is a philosophy, a mindset for how to live effectively. The Leadership Stride employs strategies and perspectives that yield results and reaffirms the benefit of effective leadership while empowering those in our family, our business, and all those whom we lead; to succeed. To manifest their potential. That is *The Leadership Stride.*

....

Eulois Cleckley

Director and CEO
Miami-Dade Department of Transportation and Public Works

Former Executive Director
Denver Department of Transportation and Infrastructure

Preface

As a volunteer in the "Watch Dog" program at the elementary school that one of my grandsons attends, I get a firsthand view of the lack of understanding of how important leadership is even at an early age. I have five adult children and fifteen grandchildren and have been active in their school years. I am an ordained minister and taught Sunday School to children for years. One thing that has never been clearer is the significance and the impact of influence on the development of today's children. I am living proof that you are never too young to understand leadership and be placed in a position of leadership. I was speaking with my ten-year-old grandson about leadership. I wanted him to realize that being a leader comes with responsibility. My grandson has been blessed with the ability to get others to follow what he was doing. This has been the case since he was a very young boy, maybe around five years old. Unfortunately, much of what they were following wasn't good. As I was educating my grandson, I remembered how I had been introduced to leadership. I had been asked to be a safety patrol officer in the second grade at my elementary school. I remember asking my teacher what a safety patrol officer was and why she'd asked me. I had seen the orange belt worn by older kids. She said that as a safety patrol officer I was to help look out for the safety of my classmates and other kids in the school. She went on to say that if someone was acting up, I was to remind them of how we conduct ourselves. I wasn't too keen on wearing that orange belt. I by far wasn't the biggest kid in my class, so correcting other kids didn't excite me either. As to why she'd asked me, she said that there was something special about me. She said, "You are always polite and respectful to everyone, and you are well-liked." I loved my teacher, so I said yes. Once I became a safety patrol officer, my being liked by everyone was certainly tested, but that's another story.

I received a call earlier this year from Irish, a friend of my mother's. This is how the call went. "Gilbert, you will never guess who asked about you the other day." I asked, "Who? Irish said Ms. Revis, your first grade teacher. Ms. Revis asked if I knew where you were and how you were doing. I said yes, that your mother and I were close friends prior to her passing and that you and my brother were still close friends." My mother's friend said, "Gilbert, she is one hundred years old. She is one hundred years old and asking about you. She said that there was something special about you and that she absolutely loved having you in her class."

I will be honest; I was literally blown away by the fact that after all these years my first grade teacher remembered me. Of all the students she had taught over all the years! It was a testament to how sharp her mind still was. The person calling said that not only was it a testament to her mind but to the impact I'd had on her. This polite and respectful little boy from Pleasant Shade, Virginia.

The next year we formed a 4-H club in our somewhat small rural community. I was asked to be one of the officers in the club. Anyone remember the 4-H club? Once again, I was chosen to fulfill a leadership role at an early age. The adults who were responsible for the 4-H club were also active in my local church. The church was another place where I had been cast into a leadership role on several occasions.

I am compelled to write *The Leadership Stride* because, as stated, I believe that one is never too young to understand the importance of leadership. It can shape our lives and provide a foundation for our choices in life, our development throughout life's experiences, and the way we impact the lives of those around us. The way we lead should reflect how we live, and the way we live should reflect what is within us. Leading the right way reaps tangible benefits and tremendous self-fulfillment. Men and women, both young and some older, are falling prey to those who operate ineffectively in the leadership arena. The Bible tells us that people perish because of a lack of knowledge. Teams perish, and like it or not, there are those in positions of authority who may not be doing it right, and we have no choice but to follow. My goal is to caution us not to adopt leadership principles that are set before us but lack effectiveness. I have heard it said often, "The leader makes the position; the position doesn't make the leader." An individual may be your leader but be very careful with whom you pattern your leadership style.

As it is in parenting, a leader has an opportunity to develop and shape someone else. That is an awesome privilege and one that should be cherished. We're not leaders just to see that tasks are completed and the job gets done. We are placed in positions of authority not to just boss people around but to mold and show others the way to lead. I challenge each of us to look in the mirror, examine how we lead, and ask the questions, "Am I the type of leader who I would want to follow? Is my only concern for the results of the numbers, or am I also concerned with the nurturing and the growth of the people?" As leaders we must remember that we are not only affecting those who we lead but those who will be led by those we lead. Our reach goes much further than what we see!

T here are hundreds and maybe even thousands of organizations that have tasted success.

The number of those organizations that were able to *maintain* that level of success decreases significantly because the rest failed to realize the importance of sustained effective leadership. Even the organizations that did consider its significance chose not to invest in creating a culture of effective leadership. On the other end of the spectrum, organizations that understand and appreciate the value of effective leadership take action to create effective leadership within the organization. You can't have an effective team with ineffective leadership. If you are to get the most out of the team, you must first get the most out of your leadership. The organizations that experience consistent success will be first to say that sustained effective leadership, coupled with the strength of an engaged team, is what not only got them to where they are but keeps them there.

The Leadership Stride is designed to enhance and further develop your leadership skills and those of your leadership team. We all know that leadership is an influence, but I say to you that leadership is *more* than an influence. Leadership is an influence in *action*.

So often organizations desire to take steps toward sustained leadership with no success. It is human nature that when we are trying to go somewhere, we take one step at a time. I'm going to use the analogy of a horse. When a horse takes a step, it's not a step. It is a stride: a coordinated movement of all the parts that were designed to help the horse move from one place to another. In any organization or on any team, there are several parts. If our goal is to take the Leadership Stride, it must be a coordinated effort involving each part of the team.

A "stride" is a long, decisive step typically covering the distance of two steps. Though the Leadership Stride is not about reducing the time to get to where we are going; it is about how far we are able to get with a single stride versus a step. For us, striding is not as instinctive as it is for the horse. We must stride purposefully. It won't happen naturally. Instinctively we take steps, not strides, as we walk. Again, the Leadership Stride does not focus on faster, but farther! Once you and your team determine that the goal is to have a people-oriented, results-driven leadership team, you must remain true to that commitment for as long as it takes. How long it takes varies based on the organization. No matter how long it takes, the goal is to not only arrive there but to do what it takes to stay there. Situations will present themselves that will challenge your direction. We know that. The question will be: Will you revert to the old, or will you remain consistent in building the new and improved? Will you choose the path that produces mediocrity or one that generates inclusion and engagement as you and your team together make the journey to sustained leadership excellence? The leadership principles highlighted in this book are illustrated in a manner that will **engage** the reader, **educate** those who will hear what *The Leadership Stride* is saying, and **empower** those who will apply these concepts on their way to sustained effective leadership. Leadership is powerful. Don't take the journey or the opportunity lightly!

CHAPTER ONE
LEADERSHIP CREDIBILITY

Character

Relatable

Engaged

Dependability

When my son was eighteen years old, he introduced me to a term called *street cred*. I thought I had an idea of what it meant, but I asked the question anyway: "What is street cred son?" He said it means that the people in the street, those who are in that lifestyle, feel that they can trust you. It means that you can be believed.

A leader in an organization doesn't have to have street cred, but they must have leadership cred or leadership credibility. Those on the team must view them as trustworthy and believable. Of course, many times the leader may not know everyone personally, but there should be someone on the team who can vouch for their trustworthiness and **dependability**. If you have street cred, it means the people in the street approve of you and consider you to be a part of their culture. If a leader is to truly connect with those they lead, the team must feel that the leader shares, at least to some degree, their values, and principles. The team must trust that the leader can relate to where they are and can represent their concerns.

When I was a new enlistee in the US army back in 1977, a group of us flew into the JFK airport in New York for basic training, or for what some call boot camp. There were about forty of us herded onto what looked like a vehicle used to transport cattle. We were packed in like sardines. The transport broke down on the approximately sixty-mile route from JFK to Fort Dix, New Jersey. It was about thirty-five degrees, as it was November in New York. By design there was no heat: another element generated by the military to make things uncomfortable for us. Those of you who have had the great experience of military training can no doubt relate to that tactic. It took three hours or so for someone to reach us and repair the vehicle. I would venture to say that at least 90 percent of us appeared to be fresh out of high school. For a moment, imagine being on a bus for three hours with complete strangers and not being allowed to talk, our minds wondering what we had gotten ourselves into, cold, hungry, and wondering if this was just another tactic by the army to get us out of our comfort zone or was it a sign that we had made the wrong choice in joining the army. We were in a place we had never been before, being yelled at, being threatened, and needing to go to the bathroom. Once we arrived at our destination and began to off-load, it was clear that some had not been able to endure our experience without Mother Nature making her call. The last few miles of our trip were almost unbearable because of the stench from the urine.

There were other new enlistees in our group, or what we learned later to be our platoon, who had previously arrived. Once we were all in formation, the drill sergeants panned the formation, looking for those who would be assigned platoon and squad leader responsibilities. They chose five of us and asked us to come to the front of the formation. No one really knew anyone, but the drill sergeants asked the platoon which of the five they would choose for platoon leader, leader of the entire group. To this day I am not sure why, out of the sixty, I was chosen. Later, however, I discovered why I was chosen to be the overall leader, or the platoon leader. Of the five, I was the only one who had been on the bus and shared the transport breakdown experience. Without even trying, I had earned leadership cred. Why? I had endured an awkward emotional experience with a group of men just beyond our teenage years. I asked a couple of the guys separately who had accompanied me on that luxurious ride why they'd chosen me. They both said the same thing in so many words. They said it was something in my eyes and my face, that though we'd all been wondering what was going on, that was different. The only thing I can think of was where my mind had been or what my thoughts had been at that time. I was present in the moment, but not consumed by the moment. Take away from my experience here that there are times when you may find yourself a part of a group that may be amid tough times or maybe even in unchartered waters. You never know at that moment what the result of that experience may be. Handle yourself appropriately. Questions. What does it mean to be present in the moment? What does it mean to not be consumed by the moment?

Be present in the moment, but not consumed by the moment. **Example:** I was very much aware of our circumstance, but what no one knew on that transporter was in that moment, my focus was on where we were, but in the backdrop was my determination to be the best soldier possible. **Note:** When those around you appear to be rattled, when circumstances seem uncertain; that is the time to reaffirm your vision and your goals within yourself. A group of men who would become very much a part of my life for the next eight weeks saw something in my disposition during a time of difficulty that caught their attention. It wasn't something I had done, but rather my mental focus on the big picture that manifested in my **disposition through a shared difficult experience.**

Leadership credibility is not easily earned in the normal process of things. It generally takes building relationships through connection. Experiencing the ups and downs, the positives, and the negatives of life as a part of a team. There has always been and will probably always be a discussion as to whether leadership ability is born in you or learned. I won't get into all that, but I will say that for me, it appears to have always been there.

As a specialist attending the US army's primary leadership school in 1980 in Bad Tölz, Germany, I once again found myself in a situation that was somewhat unusual that led to a position of greater leadership. We were one week into our five-week training period and getting ready for our first weekend pass. The weekend pass authorized us to be able to leave the post. The morning prior to our pass, the training instructor conducted an inspection and found contraband in the bathroom. The training instructor called an emergency formation and told us what he'd found and where he'd found it. He asked whose it was. Of course, no one fessed up. After a couple of minutes, the instructor told us that as a result of what happened, none of us would receive the weekend pass we were so looking forward to. It was then that I raised my hand and admitted that what had been found was mine, though it was not. I did not want to see the entire group be punished for something they'd had nothing to do with. I spent the entire weekend sweeping, mopping, and buffering floors and cleaning bathrooms. Once everyone returned, we found out who the contraband had belonged to. My fellow soldiers were so appreciative of the sacrifice I'd made on their behalf. It was then I was given the nickname "CC," short for Classy **Character**, a nickname that has stuck for many years since. Somehow the training instructor later found out that the contraband wasn't really mine. At that Sunday afternoon formation, once again I found myself responsible for the entire platoon, some that were even more senior than me in tenure and time in rank. As a note, the soldier who almost cost everyone received a real nice, what we called, "blanket party." If you've been in the military or maybe a part of another large organization much like the military, you know what is included in a blanket party. For those of you who don't know what a blanket party is, allow me to share. A blanket party is a planned affair. Everyone in the room and maybe some guests that aren't assigned to the room wait until everyone is supposed to be asleep and at a pre-determined time, enter the room of the honored guest (the one getting the "beat down"). A blanket is thrown over their head. All the invited guests begin to punch them. Very rarely was there any serious injury. Mostly a few bruises and soreness. We all have experiences in our lives in which we can choose how we react. I encourage you to look for ways "to take the high road" and be the bigger person. Leadership credibility earned through **self-sacrifice**.

I was provided an opportunity afforded by a temp service in 1992 to work in the transportation office for the biggest retailer in the world. I worked third shift along with two permanent hourly associates. As a temporary associate, I picked up the processes and quickly fit right in, though initially I thought the environment would be too intense. I reported to the front desk at the distribution center as instructed by the temp service. I received my badge and proceeded up the stairs. It was eleven p.m., and through the glass window in the door, I could see a room filled with people, all moving around somewhat frantically. It was noisy and, to be honest, a little unsettling for me. I went back downstairs to the window at the front desk, turned in my badge, and went to my car. I got inside and started the car. In my mind I wanted nothing to do with that kind of situation, but I also knew that I needed the job. The search for employment had been somewhat lengthy since our return from Germany just a couple of weeks prior. I cut the car off, went back, retrieved the badge, and went back upstairs to work. Over the next couple of months, I would be teased and laughed at because of the initiative and the serious approach I took with my duties even though I was a temporary associate. The assignment was to be a ninety-day assignment. The transportation director asked to meet with me after ten weeks or two and a half months. He told me that he'd received a lot of positive feedback from the drivers and the managers regarding me and my performance. The transportation director asked me to share my background with him. Once I had done so, he said, "We really don't have an open permanent position, but I am going to create one for you. Would you be interested?" Of course, I said yes, and the rest is history. I continued to demonstrate that same initiative and focus in my duties. There wasn't a team leader or supervisor role on the shift, but whenever things would come up or there was something extra needed, I would take the lead. It didn't seem as though anyone else would. I didn't have a title, but how many know the title doesn't make the leader anyway? If we were going to provide the customer service expected, a leader was needed in those situations. Through the initiative I demonstrated, we were able to meet, and in some cases surpass, expectations. The leadership I displayed is what is referred to today as situational leadership. The department grew so much over the next year. A supervisor position was created on another shift. I was asked to apply. I applied and was selected. I knew no one on the shift, but my leadership cred preceded me, and the transition was a success. Don't be hesitant to be the one who gets things done when others won't. Let them laugh, joke, and clown on you. It's your character that you want to demonstrate. I received leadership credibility not from disposition in shared experiences this time, and not through self-sacrifice this time, but through **self-initiative**.

As a matter of example, my pastor at my local church had no formal leadership training. The late Bishop Alfred L. Nicholson will always be one of the greatest examples of leadership credibility. The pastor was overwhelmed, tired, and, as he confessed later, almost ready to throw in the towel. He went on a cruise with his wife. During that cruise, he purchased a book by Dr. Rick Warren that challenged his perspective on leadership in ministry. Upon his return, the pastor asked the congregation who would be interested in becoming a part of the ministry's leadership team. The pastor was wise in understanding that everyone couldn't be on the leadership team, but setting expectations and realistic objectives would allow people an opportunity to disqualify themselves over a relatively short period of time, as it would turn out. We began leadership and teamwork training on Saturdays initially, then early on Sunday mornings, with Dr. John C. Maxwell as our remote facilitator. *The 21 Irrefutable Laws of Leadership* and *The 17 Indisputable Laws of Teamwork* were our resources. The pastor sat there with the team through each of the thirty-eight total sessions for almost twelve months. Not only did he attend, but he was a student hungry for knowledge and practical methods to apply what we were learning. He didn't have to, but he wanted to lead by example and benefit from what we were learning. Even though he was the pastor, he wanted to be held accountable to the same expectations as we were. He was the epitome of a great team member and a highly effective leader. I personally lived leadership credibility through shared experience, self-sacrifice, and self-initiative. Bishop Nicholson provided me with a bird's-eye view of **leadership credibility through example**. Be on alert for that leader in your life who leads through example. That one who represents genuine authentic leadership. A leader who not only talks the talks but walks the walk. If you don't have anyone in your life who fills the bill, I suggest you change your circle.

The Leadership Stride emphasizes that one can be placed in a leadership position. The role can have tremendous responsibility: tens and even hundreds of people looking to you to lead them, but the assignment itself does not necessarily come with leadership credibility. If the leader is to be effective, they must come equipped with leadership credibility. If not, they must go out and get it. Positions or titles come with authority attached, but the leader is accountable for providing credibility. Leadership credibility will compel people to follow you where none of you have ever been before!

Toolbox Alert: I challenge you to never see your present situation or circumstances bigger than your vision for yourself. Be sensitive to the moment, but when things get tough, make your vision larger. Magnify who and what you want to be. See your aspirations and goals more clearly during times of adversity. That's what I mean when I say, "Be present in the moment, but not consumed by the moment."

CHAPTER TWO
LEADERSHIP RIZZ

Refreshing

Inspiring

Zingy

Zealous

I grew up in a very rural community. The one thing that we had in our favor was that we had plenty of playmates. There were about fifteen boys within four to five years of age of each other and all within one mile. I grew up around a lot of nice guys and some maybe not so nice, so I witnessed a lot. In all my years growing up, I never experienced a kid quite like my oldest grandson. Jonathan was one of the nicest boys you'd meet most of the time. Nice at home, nice in the neighborhood, nice at church, but this one particular year when he went to school, it was one thing after the other. Talking back to the teacher, picking on other kids, and the list went on and on. I met with his teachers, and there seemed to be no rhyme or reason for the change in Jonathan's behavior. Finally, after this repeated behavior, it was decided to allow me to come to school one day and try to discreetly observe my grandson. What I discovered was that there was a certain boy in three of Jonathan's five classes. In the two classes the boy wasn't in, my grandson didn't have any issues. I realized that as this boy behaved, so did Jonathan. Why the teachers did not realize this, I am not sure. Once Jonathan got home that afternoon, I shared my observation with him. I described the other boy to him and asked who he was. Jonathan said that the boy was a friend he'd met at the start of the school year. I asked him if he knew why his behavior was different when he was around this boy. He said, "Yes." I asked why. Jonathan was direct and answered quickly. He said, "Because I wanted to be his friend. He's cool! So, I act like he acts." I'm sure you know the gist of the conversation that took place after that. Jonathan made an adjustment and didn't have any further issues at school. His teachers even commented that Jonathan became a leader in his own right, leading in a positive way. This situation reminded me of the power one person can have over another person. Jonathan got a lesson on how influence can take you to some place you don't want to be. Jonathan never lost that special knack of having others follow him. Everywhere he went, others would follow.

There are leaders who have charisma and influence and there are those who are influential. To be influential is to use your influence or charisma to serve others or change lives. At the heart of the matter is the motive or the desire of the one with the influence. Charisma is used to describe leaders who use their communication skills, persuasiveness, and charm to influence others. That charisma for the sake of the Leadership Stride, will be referred to as "rizz." *Rizz* is slang and comes from the word *charisma*: the ability to get what you want from people based on your charm, communication skills, and personality. Let us not be deceived. There are those on our teams without leadership titles or leadership duties who have tremendous influence, charisma, or rizz. It should come as no surprise that there are also those in leadership roles who have influence that goes beyond that of the senior leaders. Leadership "Rizz" is that special something, my grandson Jonathan had. Unfortunately, Jonathan was tragically murdered in February of 2023. I will never forget the leadership "Rizz" he demonstrated time and time again.

Ron, one of our company's regional directors called to share an opportunity. One that I would have never imagined would be offered to me. What made the opportunity unique was the fact that it was in fleet maintenance, an area I had no training nor knowledge in. I was told that a leader was needed, not someone who knew how to turn wrenches. I accepted the role. Upon my assignment in fleet mainte-nance as the service manager, I was quite uncomfortable; but up for the challenge. The opening was back in the facility in which I had gotten my start with the company years ago, though in a different department. Maintenance versus transportation. As I reported to the location and the new assignment, it became painfully obvious to me that I was in for an uphill battle. I felt like a fish out of water. All I'd known up to that point in my career had been regional transporta-tion and grocery transportation operations. Not only did I not know anything about maintenance operations, but the gentleman who had been temporarily running the operation, James, had applied for the role with no success. James was the individual who I would need to lean on to help navigate the learning process. Was James disappointed that he wasn't given the opportunity? Yes, but he was not bitter. At least, I didn't sense that he was. To top things off, James had grown up through the ranks; he was very knowledgeable and very well-liked by absolutely everyone on the team, and everyone on the team had seriously been hoping that he would get the opportunity. I was fortu-nate that I did not sense any hostility from James, but boy, did I sense it from the others. I didn't have to sense it in some cases. It was clear. Absolutely clear!

My predecessor had left much undone and many administrative and some operational processes out of compliance. In a short period of time, James had begun to turn much of this around. I even began to ask myself why I'd been chosen and why James had not been giv-en the position. I was very impressed with his interactions with the rest of the team, how well they responded to his direction, and how smooth things were flowing. I called my regional manager, Ron, who had made the initial call and spearheaded the interview process, to discuss some other matters. During that conversation I shared how well things were running and the upbeat morale of the team. During that exchange, I asked, "Why I was chosen for the job and not James?" The response I received will never leave me. The response was, "Yes, things are going well. James would do a fine job for where we are now." Ron went on to say, "What you don't know is that we weren't looking for a leader who could do what is expected now, but one who has the demonstrated leadership skills to lead where we are going, not where we are."

What I would experience over the next year fully exceeded my expectations. James and I went to lunch. A rather lengthy lunch, I might add. James and I had had some interactions when our paths crossed during our departments' coordination with various projects over the years, but we didn't know each other well. James told me that he'd had an opportunity to ask other leaders, drivers, and hourly associates what kind of a leader I was, but more importantly, what kind of man I was. He said the feedback he'd received had prompted him to decide to help me succeed in the transition. James was **zingy**, as he went about using his influence with each one of the team members to build a foundation for me. I was inspired by his **intentional** approach to rizz. The team trusted me because they trusted James. I was granted a degree of credibility just based on his words. James was influential in that he used his influence to serve my cause and make a positive difference on our team. Our levels of efficiency and proficiency reached great heights. I will never forget how, seemingly right before my eyes, there was a **zealous** attitude in the air that spread throughout our maintenance team. When those around us anticipated a great deal of tension and conflict on our team, there was something **refreshing** going on: two leaders, James and I, working together for the benefit of the entire group.

Just as I had been told by my regional manager, things did in fact begin to change. Corporately, processes changed. Expectations increased significantly. Operational goals were established at what appeared to be beyond reasonable levels. After about eighteen months, James was presented with an opportunity outside of the company that he couldn't turn down. The team would miss his expertise and the value he added to the team, but in the years to come, we would go on to meet every challenge. I could now begin to see why I had been chosen. The in-house processes and reports that I initiated served us well and gave us a decided advantage over some of the other maintenance facilities in the network. Soon other regional managers began to experiment with the same idea of placing leaders outside of the maintenance network to fill this key role. Sometimes it was successful. Sometimes it wasn't.

I have no doubt that I was treated to an experience with one of the most influential leaders at a time and in a role that I certainly did not expect. I remained in that role by my own choice for years. The success that I experienced, largely based on a foundation that was initially established on James's influence, would open many doors of opportunity for me.

Toolbox Alert: This experience taught me that though you have no control over how people in your new surroundings receive you or react to your selection as their new leader, you can control how you allow it to affect you. They may or may not know you. It will take time for them to accept you. You shouldn't force it. On paper you are a member of the team and their leader, but it will be up to you to become a part of them. Slowly build relationships through how you communicate and the way you embrace each member of the team. Every relationship is valuable. The relationship with the custodian is just as important as any other relationship. It is just as much your responsibility to embrace the team as it is for the team to receive you. Yes, you want to gain influence. Yes, you want to establish Rizz, but allow it to be something you use to enhance and build others. Don't use it as a tool that will only benefit you.

The Leadership Stride highlights that having influence is not enough in itself. Using that influence to serve others and make things better for someone other than yourself places you in a higher leadership class. It also provides the connection to the team you will need to have sustained effective leadership.

CHAPTER THREE
LEADERSHIP SASS

Syntactically

Awesome

Style

Sheet

Upon my arrival in August 2001 to one of our company's southeastern locations as the new general transportation director, the first thing I discovered was that the four departments within transportation were operating and striving for goals that were beneficial within their respective department but did not create a winning formula for the entire group. If we were going to attain new heights, I knew that would have to change.

I had previously asked each department leader to prepare a business presentation that outlined their prior year's performance, their current year goals, and where they were to date on those objectives. I met with each department leader individually as they went over their presentations. I didn't share a lot of feedback. I did more listening than talking, which is not a bad idea when you're getting to know your leadership team. Once I had met with each of the four departments, I scheduled an off-site two-day meeting that was to take place within the next two weeks. During that meeting, each of the department leaders was asked to present to the team what they had previously presented to me. At the conclusion of the presentations, I asked one simple question of each of them: "How does the achievement of your goals impact the other departments on the team?" There were a couple of leaders who offered a perspective on how a goal here and there affected the other departments, but for the most part, no real solid connections had any significant impact. It was at that point that I decided to offer an example of the collaborative effort that would be required for us to enhance our effectiveness as a team.

One of the departments that comprised the transportation operation at this location was what we called during that day a Center-Point. A CenterPoint was a consolidation dock. This one had thirty-two dock doors. There were others across the nation that were larger and some smaller. Less than truckload (LTL) freight would be brought into CenterPoint. Partial loads from vendors in South Carolina, North Carolina, and Virginia were consolidated into full loads destined for locations all over the country, from New York to California. One of the other departments within our transportation group was our transportation office. There were 200 drivers and 160 trucks delivering to stores in the same areas where third party companies were being paid a "pretty penny," as my granddad would say, for picking up our company's freight destined for the CenterPoint. Not all, but many of the trailers were returning from deliveries to our stores empty or with no freight or product. Without getting into the weeds too much, once we delivered to our stores, there was no longer any revenue being generated. The trip back to the terminal was at the local transportation office's expense. There were some occasions where we could find a full truckload that was shipped from a vendor near our delivery location back to our distribution center or maybe to a distribution center within 150 miles or so. Doing this would decrease the number of empty miles and generate revenue. CenterPoint's goal was to ensure expeditious pickup of less than truckload freight from the vendors, bring it into the dock, create full loads, and ship them out as quickly as possible. There hadn't been a lot of connection between the transportation office's goal of reducing empty miles by having our fleet transport some of the less than truckload freight that a third party was moving. It meant that our drivers had to go to multiple vendors' locations to do so sometimes. That was a change to our way of conducting business, but we worked our way through it. The two leaders of the two departments came to the realization that it would be in the best interest of the entire team to strategize how they could work together to positively impact the overall mission without significantly compromising the success that the CenterPoint was achieving. I departed the meeting, but prior to my leaving, I challenged the group to create objectives that would require them to work together for the enhancement of the overall operation. To say that the work that happened that day catapulted us to heights I had quite honestly not envisioned is an understatement. I didn't realize it then, but what we created that day is now, according to the Leadership Stride, was Leadership SASS. Let's dig into it.

Merriam-Webster says the meaning of SASS is bold rudeness or a lack of respect, sometimes considered playful, appealing, or courageous. That's the negative side of the meaning of the word. In the world of computers, SASS is the most mature, stable, and powerful professional-grade CSS extension language in the world. CSS is a computer language that forms the foundation of the basis for what's communicated. SASS is short for Syntactically Awesome Style Sheets. What Does Syntactically Awesome Style Sheets mean? Syntactically Awesome Style Sheets (SASS) is an extension to Cascading Style Sheets (CSS) that adds more features, stability, and depth on top of CSS. SASS controls how the computer language (or CSS) appears on websites as they are viewed. Cascading is to pour or flow downward. Style sheets are a type of template file consisting of a standardized look or appearance.

In the Leadership Stride, the acronym SASS has an even more profound effect. Let us break this down and consider its impact on an organization. The prefix *syn–* means *together* or *joined*. The word *tactically* is to have carefully planned actions that are designed to achieve a specific end. In the Leadership Stride, *syntactically* describes the process of multiple departments coming together, establishing actions within each department that link or connect to increase the effectiveness of the entire team. The plans or processes lead to the success of the entire team and not just certain aspects of it. The mission is achieved in excellence. SASS creates a perspective within the team and from those looking on, of oneness and unity. Oneness that defeats one's efforts to protect one's own at the expense of the whole. SASS creates a sort of filter, a flow through if you will. As priorities are adjusted and as changes within the customer base occur or even changes within the organization's structure take place, these changes must flow through SASS. Levels of growth are attained that provide a sense of awe. The Leadership Stride shares that an organization's foundation is strengthened not by the success of one or two components of the team, but the entire team collectively.

An organization's leadership should reflect and demonstrate the culture and the vision of the organization, no matter the specific goals of the individual departments within the organization. There must be a point, a common ground, where shared objectives and valued principles within the leadership team come together to support the fundamentals of what the organization is or is to become. One department shouldn't be focused on the objectives that only benefit their group and have little or no regard for the other areas on the team. The adage, "We are getting ours" has no place in a successful organization or on an effective leadership team.

....

Toolbox Alert: When attempting to create oneness within the leadership team, as the leader, don't be so quick to do all the talking. Listen more than talk at first. We have two ears and one mouth. Use them proportionately during this initial building process. Provide an example as I did with the LTL freight in this chapter. Assign the other team leaders the task of creating shared goals that benefit everyone rather than creating and dictating these goals yourself. Be a resource if you need to, not the creator. Let them do the work. What you will find is that in the process of working through this method, comradery and cohesiveness that did not exist previously will materialize.

Leadership SASS elevates the organization beyond expectations and places the team on the journey from good to great.

Opportunity

Potential

Transfer

Inspire

Connect

Significant

I will use the word *optics* here rather than *vision*, though much of what you will read in this chapter will be vision related. Vision is something every leader must have. That's not new to anyone. Without vision, there is no clear direction or path for the team or organization. *The Leadership Stride* encourages leaders to consider an additional approach to the concept of vision. Optics is defined as the aspects of an action, policy, or decision and how it is perceived by the public. As a leader shares or casts a vision, he is seizing an **opportunity** to set a course for the organization. Vision should be given thorough and careful planning. The leader should not be quick in determining a vision for the organization. Let me clarify. Though optics are important and should be considered by the leader, they shouldn't be given more weight by the leader than the vision itself. As stated, typically when people think of *optics*, they are referring to how outsiders will perceive something. It is also **significant** how those on the team view the vision. What are their optics?

There are multiple levels throughout the organization. Certain questions should be asked: How will the vision be understood by each group on the team? Will the vision be perceived in the same way by each component of the team? Does the vision take into consideration the culture of the organization? Are the principles and values of the organization captured in the vision?

The vision should be authentic. It can say the same thing or bear a resemblance to that of other organizations, but the leader must make the vision their own. It should be authentic or genuine in that the vision should be from the heart of the leader or the leadership team. Does this direction really take us where we want to go, and is this how we want to get there? Does it **inspire** and engage our team members? What may work for one organization may not work for yours.

Ultimately, the senior leader is responsible for vision. The leader should communicate the vision both in writing and verbally. Many times, optics are derived from the way the vision is communicated. Once the vision is communicated, the leader should be certain to ensure that the vision has been **transferred**. A moment of transparency here: I have been fortunate to have great visions for my teams over the years that are communicated annually, as with most organizations. There was one year when I was admittedly extremely proud of the vision. As always, I gathered my inner circle and shared it. I instructed each of them to shape the vision within their departments based on the responsibilities and functions within those areas. I cautioned them to ensure that the essence of the vision was not lost, but I failed in that I did not require them to share that adaptation with me prior to moving forward. The plan was to have an all-inclusive grassroots meeting including all departments and all team members. I wanted the entire team to come to that meeting having heard their vision from their department and prepared to provide feedback. Prior to that meeting, I was approached by one of our team members with a question regarding his department's vision. Just let me say that what had been transferred to that department was quite a bit different from what I thought everyone had left the room with that day when I'd initially shared the vision the department leaders. I reached out to the leader of the department and asked him to share what he had gathered from our vision casting meeting. He had missed the essence of the vision and missed it significantly. I don't know how. He couldn't tell me how he had gotten so far off the mark! What I learned that day was that when casting a vision, not only do you have to verbally express it and talk about it, and not only should you write it and make it plain, but you must also verify that vision transferred. As leaders we can't rush through the vision component. It is too important. Develop a timetable that will provide an opportunity to verify vision transfer. I suggest 30 to 60 days after vision casting to ensure the entire team understands their role in vision.

....

TOOLBOX ALERT: Allow me to introduce you to Vision Evoked **Potential**. (VEP) is a medical term that pertains to the eye or one's vision. The word evoked means to bring to one's mind or bring to one's consciousness. In the medical world visual evoked potential is a vision that occurs because of a visual stimulus, usually an electric pulse. The Leadership Stride challenges the leader's ability to stimulate a response in those that they lead. That stimulus occurs when the team members see themselves in the vision of the leader and their potential is now revealed to them. They have a picture in their minds of where they fit in and how they can contribute. Once a team member can see themselves in the leader's vision, it serves as the electric pulse in the medical arena that the eye needs to have successful VEP. VEP is needed in an organization as well. The leader must be able to stimulate a team member's perception of their potential in the vision and how they **connect**. The leader must ensure that the organization invests the time to have an individual conversation with those on the team. Of course, the size of the organization may hinder one person from having these one-on-one conversations, but the senior leader should have this dialogue with those in their immediate circle and require the discussion to take place at all levels. Mandate that feedback capturing the gist of those conversations be provided to the leadership team.

As stated, ultimately the senior leader is responsible for vision. The leader should communicate the vision both in writing and verbally and ensure the vision has been transferred. As we are speaking about optics, let me ask this question. What are the optics surrounding your leadership vision? Do you know how the team perceives your vision? No matter what the level of leadership, every leader should have a vision. Be mindful that this vision should not supplant the senior leader's vision. Your vision should reinforce the vision of the leader.

Be true to the process of effective vision and successful optics. It will be an ongoing endeavor. Are you a leader that monitors, manages, and tries to control the reaction of your team through planned group meetings, surveys, and suggestion boxes? Or are you a leader that stays close to your team through personal relationships established by consistent connection. The Leadership Stride suggests that through connection leaders are aware of the emotions of team members before they've had an opportunity to fester and have a negative impact on other members of the team.

Moments

Intangibles

Necessary

Determined

The days when a leader could show up, find out what needs to be done, tell people to do it, and call their job complete once it's done are long gone. Regretfully, there are still some leaders who have this mindset. Leaders who fulfill their responsibilities as leaders with that thought process negatively impact the culture of an organization. An organization striving to create a people-oriented, results-driven leadership team cannot allow that to continue. Every leader impacts our culture, and if culture is important, training our leaders to have a different mindset is a great investment. We must be **determined** to help our leaders become leaders of thought.

A leader must consider more than workload. Of course, safety is always the number one priority. Nothing is more important than a culture of safety. *The Leadership Stride* requires that leaders must now consider how to keep those they lead engaged, rewarded, and feeling like they are a part of the process. There may be only so much we can do to reward through compensation, but the value of a rewarding experience lasts longer than money. Money in most cases is still king when an individual is considering their workplace, but there are some intangibles that can separate your organization from others. The personality of the leadership team, workplace behavior, and the energy in the environment can sway whether a current team member stays. It also influences prospective team members as well.

One area in which a leader should think differently is regarding processes. We've all heard the phrase, "Inspect what you expect." You tell people what the process is, show them how the process works, and be sure to check to make sure that the process is being completed properly. *The Leadership Stride* challenges the mind of the leader to consider more. The leader should not only inspect but assess.

Measure and analyze to determine if the process as it is completed presently is still the most efficient method. To inspect is to check for conformity. Are we doing it the way we said it is to be done? To assess is to measure results. Are we getting a return on the investment? We say that the value of the current process is one thing, but what is the value of the process according to the others on the team and to those we serve, the customers? Let's take the assessment phase further. Is the team committed to the process because we believe in the results, or are we complying with the process out of obligation? Do we want our processes to make a difference and add value, or do we want to continue to do it that way because that's the way we've always done it?

An example of a process with one of my previous organizations where an assessment was **necessary** was our orientation and reorientation process. HR had scheduled reorientation for sixty days after the initial orientation for new associates. There was a team of leaders who conducted the reorientation. At this point associates were not leaving the company, but the excitement, enthusiasm, and appreciation for being a part of the organization was dwindling significantly. My leadership team and I gathered feedback from those involved in the sixty-day reorientation. After speaking to the reorientation team, we discovered that the company was making assumptions that were not the reality for the new associates. By the time the sixty days rolled around, things were in some cases already going in the wrong direction. We began to analyze the specifics of what was being covered in the reorientation and discovered that those topics were as they should be. The next item we verified was to see if the sixty-day reorientations were occurring in a timely manner. Yes, in each case they were conducted as they should've been. We expected those results. We could've been satisfied with that, but the question remained. What was going wrong? What was happening within sixty days that caused our new associates to lose excitement and gratefulness to be a part of our team? Locally, within our department, we decided to start our own reorientation, but at the thirty-day mark. It didn't replace HR's sixty-day orientation, but the thirty-day reorientation provided us an opportunity to correct some things earlier in the process and to address some concerns of the new team members prior to escalation. The thirty-day reorientation that we conducted within our internal department proved to positively impact the results of the overall department's sixty-day reorientation. The feedback received in the sixty-day reorientation was much more positive. We knew that the sixty-day reorientation was not providing the quality we anticipated. We just didn't know why. As we discovered, it happened too late in the associates' ninety-day window. Inspecting what we expected was good, but if we had not assessed the results of the inspection and spoken with those conducting the reorientation, the company would've lost key personnel within six months. No doubt the implementation of the thirty-day reorientation proved to be successful. There were more than a few occasions where the adjustment of the timing of reorientation helped the organization decrease turnover. It was said more than once by new team members that they would have left with the previous process in place.

Another way for us to challenge the thought process of our leaders is to focus on teachable moments.

How many have heard the term "coaching by walking around" (CBWA)? It is basically designed to ensure that, as leaders, we spend time in the work environment interacting with those we lead. I have seen CBWA add value to the culture, and I have seen it have the adverse effect. Some leaders unfortunately view CBWA as an occasion to catch someone not doing it right when it should be about moments that build relationships. It is really designed to strengthen the relationships with those we lead. Leaders are to search for "teachable moments." Three things must be present to have a teachable moment: there must be a subject or topic, someone ready to learn, and someone ready to teach. There is a fourth thing, however, that increases engagement. The teacher must be not only willing to teach but also prepared to learn. Now not only has the skill set of the team been elevated, but the voice of the learner has been afforded an opportunity to add to the experience. What that team member has to say may be something you have heard before, but can you hear it again for the first time? Let us include our entire team in the learning process, even leadership.

The last area of focus regarding the leadership mind is usually an area of great controversy within organizations. Accountability within the team weighs heavily on the culture. Many times, the value of accountability is underserved. Accountability cannot be a one-way street. If it is, there is only one direction our organization can go. It may be gradual, but that kind of culture will not create the results we are after. If we are to truly desire to take the Leadership Stride, we must be accountable to those we lead, accountable in that we allow those we lead a forum to tell us how we are doing. This level of communication and accountable behavior creates an atmosphere for growth.

As leaders we have various levels of authority. We defeat ourselves when we try to implement accountability solely from a place of authority rather than a place of connection. So many times, I have heard, "You may not respect me, but you're going to respect my position." What a one-sided perspective! When those we lead respond to us because of the power of our position rather than the partiality toward our presence, we lose. Partiality means that those we lead value the relationship we have formed. Relationships are created through the investment of time and caring. Relationships produce favor versus fear. We win when those we lead are compelled to respond based on who we are rather than what we are. What have we accomplished if our team members respond out of compliance or obligation because of what our position says we are? Our level of influence must be more than our position titles!

Toolbox Alert: No process is too sacred to be reviewed, analyzed, and adjusted if need-be. Involve the team in evaluating or reviewing your processes. If we can do that, we can create a sense of ownership that will be required for sustained effective leadership. Get your leadership team to engage in having a daily presence in the work environment of those they lead. The feedback they receive in that setting will be much more valuable than that gained any other way. Practice accountability that will operate on a two-way street. Doing so will foster a level of trust that is rarely found in most organizations. Design a leadership team who can thrive from constructive feedback, not run from it. There is nothing wrong if there is a process that needs to be reconsidered, an aspect of the work environment that needs to be addressed, or even a personnel issue that requires attention. You want that feedback!

The Leadership Stride should provoke leaders to reevaluate how we lead, assess what we inspect, teach us how to lead and learn from those we lead, and help us understand that accountability is more than the consequences of not doing something right.

CHAPTER SIX
LUCID LEADERSHIP

Link

Understood

Courage

Impact

Dynamic

In 2005 the company transitioned from our transportation fleet delivering only slow-moving items (TVs, motor oil, dishwashing liquid, and so on) through our network to also transporting merchandise that moved through our centers to our store shelves and out the front door quickly (paper towels, toilet paper, water, and the like). I was fortunate to provide regional support during that transition to our offices in Georgia, South Carolina, North Carolina, and Virginia. One common theme in nearly all the locations I visited with team members was a lack of clarity regarding leadership. Many said that they did not understand their leadership teams or that their leadership team wasn't clear about certain issues. Not once did I think the leaders at any of these locations were hiding anything or purposefully being evasive. It was a matter of a lack of transparency and maybe some mixed signals. I suggested to the leadership at these locations to schedule a meeting to share the basics of the transition. Take the time to explain what prompted the decision to move in a new direction and to find ways to create additional security within the team. The unknown presents an opportunity for discord. Of course, not everyone acted on the suggestion. It was clear, however, who did.

The word *lucid* means expressed clearly, easy to understand, or comprehensible. Lucid leadership is a leadership team's demonstrated ability to share concise and clear information with the team from an honest and sometimes vulnerable place—vulnerable in that you may not have all the answers yet, and sometimes not knowing all the answers can make you seem less than knowledgeable and insecure. When information is shared accurately and timely, the leader runs the risk of questions being asked for which they may not be able to answer. It takes courage. If the leader is lucid and acts from a place of credibility, they build trust and **connection** in the team. If the leader does not have credibility, then the risk may be too great. That is why Dr. John C. Maxwell shares in *the 21 Irrefutable Laws of Leadership* the Law of Solid Ground: A leader must have some coins or change in their pocket. They have done enough things right that if they make an error or have a moment in which they don't have all the pieces to the puzzle in the right places yet, when it appears that leader may not be on top of something, the leader can spend some of that change. In other words, the leader will not lose their credibility or the trust of the team. The Law of Solid Ground goes on to say that when a leader does things right, they put change or coins in their pocket. When mistakes are made or during times of uncertainty, it will cost the leader, but if the leader has change to spend, they can afford the cost. Yes, they will lose some of those coins or change. The goal is to generate more as the leader continues to lead consistently and effectively. Do you have any change or coins in your pocket?

Transparency breeds trust and understanding. To say that a leader is transparent does not mean that they give no regard for what they say or how they say it. A leader must always measure what is revealed about who they really are and how they really feel. There is a balance. Transparency in an organization **impacts** the leader, the team, and the mission.

Leader impact. What is transparency in the Leadership Stride? It is leadership's demonstration of openness in the workplace, sharing both the positive and the negative. When a leader has a reputation of being knowledgeable and experienced, they are respected and honored. As we move toward people-oriented, results-driven leadership, the **dynamic** of transparency solidifies the connection and the reputation of the leader even more. Lucid leadership serves as a link between the team and the human side of the leader. Transparency is a risk, but so is withholding impactful information from the team. Everyone does not need to know everything; I agree. So many times, in my experience with every organization I have been a part of, there has been information that leaks out to the team. Once that information leaked out, instantly the trustworthiness of the leadership team was lost. Speculation began, and with speculation came rumors, and with rumors came conflict, and with conflict came dissension in the ranks of our team. Soon team engagement was compromised, and turnover rate increased. With turnover came increased cost to hire and train. With increased cost came a loss of profit, and a loss of profit affected our ability to reward our team members and eventually had an impact on our customers.

Team impact. Leaders are not only respected because of their expertise, but now the foundation for building stronger relationships is in place. The leader is now more approachable. They are more relatable. The American Physiological Association found that only 52 percent of team members feel their leadership is transparent. A team that is more informed and not kept in the dark feels like they can be trusted. They feel as though they are valued as part of the solution process and not just impacted by it.

Mission impact. A team that knows it can share honest feedback without penalty can be challenging, but it can also be so rewarding. A workplace environment where the team can openly communicate yields greater and improved productivity because the whole team is involved. Leadership transparency can generate faster and more effective outcomes to issues or opportunities.

Air and water are transparent in nature. Let us view both through the lens of the Leadership Stride. The **air**, or the atmosphere in the work environment, is ever so important. Having experience in a culture that fostered transparency and those that did not, I can respect its impact on the team. Team members must feel like they have the freedom to express themselves and feel comfortable doing so. A culture that bridles the mouth of the team not only creates a hostile environment, but it also stifles the growth of the organization. Members of the leadership team should encourage honesty and be prepared to respond in the right way to the perspectives of the team. An environment or atmosphere like this cannot just be talked about and paraded around as an advertisement banner for recruiting purposes, but it must be evident and apparent to team members as well as those on the outside looking in. The actual air quality in the workplace is increasingly important to the health of the team members. It is also important that the team perform or produce in an air or an atmosphere complete with freedom of expression.

Water flows freely to wherever there are no obstacles or hindrances. Communication in the workplace should flow freely as well. An organization must discover how communication is consistently and accurately relayed throughout the team. We are all familiar with the exercise in which you tell one person something, and by the time it gets to the last person, many times the message is not what it started out as. Leaders can try to prevent that from happening through ensuring that firstly, the leaders are all communicating the same thing. Secondly, during our interactions with the rest of the team, verify which message was received.

Toolbox Alert: A lack of effective communication is an issue that all organizations struggle with. Most often when we think of communication in the workplace, we typically focus on communication from the top down or from the bottom up. Excellence in communication, or lucid communication, occurs when communication on the team is synonymous across the organization (360-degree communications), not just vertical (up and down). Additionally, excellence in communication is achieved when it is known whether communication is official or unofficial. It may not be true, but it is still good to know what's being communicated among the team—not the rumor mill, but conversations relative to the workplace.

Again, to be lucid is to be understood clearly. As the leader, your message to the team is always clearer when the team is familiar with the messenger. Don't be a stranger to the team. I challenge you to not be a figurehead but a real person to those you lead. Find ways to interact with the team. What are their interests? Outside of work, what is important to them? If we can touch their hearts, we can get their help.

The Leadership Stride reminds us that just because you are the leader, it does not mean you have to put up a wall that prevents the team from getting a glimpse of who you are as a person. A little transparency will help bridge the gap that often exists between leadership and the team.

CHAPTER SEVEN
LEADERSHIP CULTURE AGENT

Attitude

Growth

Environment

New

Transformation

I t is not a coincidence that the chapter on culture agents is one of the longest chapters in the book, second only to chapter one, *Leadership Cred*. The length of both chapters is indicative of how significant leadership credibility and culture agents are to a successful shift in an organization's culture.

What is culture? We hear this word so often. Culture is the *shared* values, belief systems, and attitudes, along with what those on the team or in the workplace believe to be true about where they work. There are a lot of organizations that advertise or would have others believe that the culture of the organizations is one thing when in fact it is something different. Could it be that leadership really believes what they are communicating about the culture of the organization and that they are out of touch with the reality of the culture that exists? Yes, it could be possible. It is also possible that leadership may be underestimating the value of culture and underappreciating the impact it has on the success and growth of the organization.

As a service manager in a truck shop for the first time, I found there were many areas and concerns that I wanted to address. Would

I choose an area that would be easy to build momentum in, or would I choose one that would be difficult, one that would allow me to "flex my muscles," so to speak? To show those on the outside looking in what I was capable of? I decided to go with neither one that was easy nor one that would be difficult—or at least I didn't think it would be difficult. I chose one that I felt would be most impactful for the team. I truly believe that a clean and organized **environment** affects the **attitude** of the team. I wanted to introduce something into the culture that could help serve as a foundation for what was to come. With that said, I set expectations as to how the truck shop was to look while work was being performed and at the end of shift. I did expect to receive some pushback, but not to the degree that I did. Technicians and even my leadership team were unreceptive to the ask. As I stated earlier, my leadership team started out as technicians, so I should not have been surprised. Both groups felt as though the expectations were unrealistic. Of course, they attributed my unrealistic standards to the fact that I was not reared in a shop maintenance environment. I heard everything from, "This is a truck shop; it is supposed to be dirty," to "It is just going to get dirty again in a matter of minutes; we are not eating off the floor; we are repairing trucks." These were the comments of our technicians. Those of my supporting leadership team were not quite as bad, though they seemed to also struggle with my detailed focused on housekeeping and cleanliness. I made it the primary topic for the next leadership meeting. I asked each of the four of them to give one reason why they thought the direction was overkill. To their surprise, I did not offer any rebuttal to their reasonings. I challenged them to give the expectation one month, and then we could revisit the expectation. I also asked them to monitor how they felt when they themselves started the shifts and how their teams felt. I required each of them to come to that meeting a month later and provide two reasons this time as to why they felt the expectation was too high. To their surprise, there was only one reason that could be provided. They all had the same reason: it took too much time. It was then that I introduced them to my plans for a culture shift. It was my turn to talk about my reasons for the housekeeping expectation.

If a person takes pride in how their workplace looks, if they invest some energy and time into making it better, though "better" can mean something different to some, it creates a sense of ownership in the appearance of the work area. If we could do that, we would be on our way to getting them to care about the atmosphere in which they worked—not just in cleanliness but in the character of the team. The road to a culture of team engagement would begin with these four leaders. I didn't expect all four would become cultural agents, but I did expect all four to be true to the ask, and they were. As it would turn out, they opted to keep the cleaning and housekeeping expectations. The leaders refined some of the processes and reduced some of the time it took without compromising the quality. They were engaged! There were comments made by visitors from other maintenance shops complimenting us on how good our shop looked. Only one of the four leaders was unable to truly grasp this new approach. The other three embraced this initial phase of our culture change and were extremely beneficial as together we began to change the culture of the department. No, it didn't happen overnight, but we were well on our way, though it was just one stride. Before we get into what a culture agent is, let us talk a little more about culture. Culture is the catalyst to get the results you desire. If it is your desire for a people-oriented, results-driven leadership team, if you can find the method to ignite culture, it can be the primary element to forming the bridge between mediocrity and superiority.

As leaders we must decide if this difference-maker called "culture" will work for us or against us. Many of you have heard the phrase "change agents." Change agents are those who help to facilitate a change in processes or methods. They help to correct or fix problems or issues. They are more task oriented. This sort of change is referred to as *reformation*. Reformation primarily affects external elements. *The Leadership Stride* specifies that cultural agents are needed to create change below the surface, beyond the nuts and bolts: the essence of what makes an organization what it is. Cultural agents are those who are willing and able to challenge the perspective of those they lead. They can generate a different thought process and consider and respond to those perspectives that threaten the transition to a new and improved culture. Culture agents are more thought-oriented than task-oriented. The primary focus is not what is done but the thought process behind it. They are more focused on **transformation** versus reformation. Cultural agents are those who recognize the need to experience a different culture. They are willing to embrace the **new** culture and forego comfort and convenience for the sake of transcending from the old to the new.

Cultural agents are those who can and are willing to teach and exhibit the desired values and principles across an adverse environment. Their tenure with the organization, their backgrounds, and their skill sets will be diverse. They are supportive of the new perspective and the new processes. They are our coaches on the field promoting, teaching, demonstrating, and paving the way for others. *The Leadership Stride* compels the leader to promote a change not in method but in mindset to affect the culture.

Culture agents must embrace the culture shift and are critical to the success of the transition. They are willing to get uncomfortable and are willing to be inconvenienced for the sake of the team. They must be willing to meet the team where they are, help them grasp the benefits of the new culture, and be a sounding board for the naysayers. There will be those who will be verbal and uncooperative. Culture agents are living examples of empathy and selflessness, and they must be first partakers. They must be ready to absorb some blows to their egos. The people-oriented, results-driven leader must put the task and the target before the luxury of traditionalism. The way we've always done it can't be the "mantra."

Culture agents are attentive and recognize the needs of the team as the transition is underway. Culture agents communicate the needs of the team to the appropriate level of leadership and are willing to be a part of the solution once a determination is made. Culture agents must be alert to the temperature of the team and be able to discern what is not obvious on the surface. *The Leadership Stride* requires that leaders speak the language and understand what the team is saying and why they are saying it. They must be filters. Receive the reluctance and negativity and exchange it with vision to help those we lead see the return on the investment on the journey to sustained effective leadership.

I was elevated to general transportation manager in Fayetteville, North Carolina. I was responsible for over 180 fleet drivers, eight other leaders, and thirty hourly associates. The leadership team there was coasting, going through the motions. It needed an infusion. A culture change was desperately needed. Upon my arrival, the standard practice was for those with seniority to fill the leadership roles on day shift and those more junior, the night shift. There was a critical leadership role being filled by someone doing just enough to get by in a role that, if capitalized on, could add significant revenue to the operation. Let's call him leader number one. There was a much more junior leader on the night shift who had gone to college for logistics. Let's call him leader number two: an impressive young man who was wasting away completing reports, tying up loose ends, and so on during the night shift. I knew what needed to be done, but I had to do it in a way that wouldn't kill leader number one and cause turmoil to the entire team. I shared with my corporate leader what I needed to do. He wasn't crazy about the idea initially because it went against the grain of what had been traditionally done within the transportation department. He eventually gave me the green light with some conditions. We had to improve revenue by at least 15 percent within sixty days. Rather than make the personnel and shift change immediately, I issued a challenge to leader number one to increase revenue by 15 percent in thirty days. I didn't tell him what the consequence would be if the goal wasn't achieved. The goal was not achieved, nor was it taken seriously in my opinion. We made a change in schedule. Leader number one moved from first shift to second shift and leader number two moved from first shift to second shift. The energy level and the passion of the leader number two ignited those who worked in that area. New life was breathed into the 3 associates that worked in that area of the department. They proactively engaged in new aspects of the business and the results surprised us all. After sixty days, revenue was up 30 percent. Leader number two stayed with the company a couple of years and then moved on to greener pastures. He is now the Director and CEO of public works in Dade County in Miami and has done extremely well in his career. I am appreciative and grateful of his writing the Foreword for this book. We speak often, and he attributes much of his success to the opportunity that was provided to him when was a very young man. He often states that I was the first leader to show him what true leadership courage was. He says I had the courage to make a move that was unpopular, but the method used shifted the culture of the department. What was even more impactful was the courage the change provided to others on the team to make decisions within their areas of responsibility, decisions that they had been reluctant to make because of fear—moves or adjustments that should've been made long ago. I was the first of many culture agents who were born during my tenure there. Many of those leaders who were there and witnessed the transformation of our team went on to other higher leadership roles within and outside of the company.

Toolbox Alert: As the leader you must decide and communicate what kind of culture you want to the leadership team. Identify those leaders who grasp and embrace the new culture vision. Realize those leaders who have the "grit" to demonstrate that culture in the face of opposition and resistance. Know the leaders on your team who you can trust to be conduits who will relay expectations to the team and share feedback with you as to what the team's expectations and needs are.

The Leadership Stride realizes that culture agents are just as important to the success of a culture shift as the culture itself. The shift can't be done effectively without them!

Tact

Real

Unselfishly

Engagement

The word *true* is to base something on facts and reality. I have seen so many leaders over the years lead based on what others say leadership is rather than what is within them and how their leadership training and experiences have developed. Leaders adjust how they lead, but because it is not genuine or authentic, they struggle with consistency and effectiveness. Please don't misunderstand. I do think it is necessary to adapt leadership styles based on the specifics of a situation. The problem that I see is that leaders try to lead from a place that is not within them. Promotions and elevations are indications of success, but every opportunity for advancement may not take us to the place of intersection. This place of intersect is what *The Leadership Stride* refers to as *leadership true*. An intersection is a point where two or more things intersect or meet. Leadership true is the intersection where a leader's values, beliefs, and principles come together and meet the requirements of the role. If a leadership role or position does not have an intersection, it is a recipe for disaster. Well, maybe *disaster* is a strong word, but if a leader is in a place of authority, and the essence of who they are and what they believe is in constant conflict with their duties and responsibilities, it is miserable. I speak from personal experience. To be true to who you are is to be real.

As the leader of a department with an organization, I found myself in a situation where I was quite uncomfortable. The senior leadership changed while I was in my role, and with that change unfortunately came a change in values and principles. Our department had experienced significant improvements in the two years I had been the leader. Had we obtained all the goals and expectations of leadership? No, but we were close. I mean, we were *really* close. We received a 98 percent score on our annual audit, we'd improved processes, and customer satisfaction was at an all-time high. The new senior leader requested a one-on-one meeting with me. During that meeting he asked me when I thought my department would complete a project in which we had a nine-month timetable for completion. Mind you, we had only been engaged in the project for four months. We were running ahead of schedule due to the hard work of the team. Our plan was to complete the assignment two months ahead of schedule. I shared with the new leader when the assignment would be finished and how well the team was doing with the timetable. He then asked if we could complete the project in just two more months. The senior leader said that if we could meet this new expectation, it could mean a promotion and greater compensation for me. He wanted what had started out as a nine-month project to be completed in six months. Selfishly, I needed the money and the promotion would really be nice as well. Unselfishly, I knew that if we were to meet that expectation, I would have to ask the team to commit more time to the project, which would mean additional sacrifices on top of those they were already making. It would mean less time for their personal commitments. My response was that I would need to meet with the team and get back to him in two days. This conversation took place on Friday. The supervisor gave me until the end of the day the following Monday. Though the conversation came across as if it were an ask, it was not really. So I had a couple of days to provide an answer that I knew immediately would change my life and the lives of my team.

Let me share a little bit about the team. There were eleven members including myself, two junior leaders, and eight hourly team members. One of the supervisors had coached youth football for ten years. For the sake of this book, let's refer to him as Mike. Two of the other team members were hourly and managed a dance studio for teenage girls. Again, for the sake of the book, Amber and Jasmine. We'd adjusted the work schedule as we began the project. It required each team member to work one Saturday a month, and all team members were to work three hours overtime each week. Of course, the other team members had personal considerations as well, but those are the ones I will speak of in this chapter.

I had never seen Mike in action coaching his football team. As timing would have it, I had promised him I would come to this weekend's game. I'd heard Mike was a good coach and well-respected by others associated with the team, but I was really impressed with the manner in which he handled everything that a coach is supposed to manage during a game. His demeanor was consistently positive, including the way he responded to some of the hecklers in the crowd, but most of all in the way he encouraged those little boys when things didn't go so well. After the game I made my way to Mike to share how proud I was of him. I got to him just in time to hear the postgame talk he gave his team. The team had lost the game, but I learned a great deal about Mike. I saw how passionate he was about making a difference in the lives of these boys, teaching them not just football but tidbits about life and overcoming obstacles. Much of what he said resonated with me. Why? Because some of the things he said to them were the same things I'd say to my team at work. Mike looked at me and blinked as he was talking to the team. I guess he had been listening after all!

I had seen Amber and Jasmine's dance classes perform over the years. I had marveled at what they were able to do with those girls. The age groups of the girls who they worked with were between the ages of fifteen to nineteen. A couple of my daughters and granddaughters had learned to dance because of Amber and Jasmine's dance school. When one of my daughters became an adult, she developed a passion for teaching other teen girls and chose to do so with her own dance class. There was a dance competition coming up, and so were the playoffs for Mike's football team. That Saturday and Sunday I toiled with asking the team to adjust to the new expectation. I felt in my heart that they would do it, but I kept thinking about how it would affect their personal lives and the lives of the children they worked with. I was inspired by the engagement of my team members in their communities. I realize that as a leader there are times we must make tough choices. Choices that produce consequences that negatively impact team members. The loss of peace that the leader has in those situations is a reminder that effective leadership does not require a loss of compassion and sensitivity. You can be decisive without being detrimental. That is to say that there are times when a choice must be made. The choice can be definite without tearing down the team. Do leaders still take one for the team? This kind of selfless leadership is rarer these days.

As requested, I got back to my new supervisor within the time frame expected. I knew how important and professional tact is in communication, particularly communication that may not be received well. I told my supervisor that my team was already stretched in meeting the seven-month completion window we had placed upon ourselves and that anything more would require more overtime and personal sacrifice. He proceeded to inform me that we didn't have an option. He had already told the president of the company about the revised completion date. He went on to tell me that if I couldn't do it, he could find someone who could. Well, unfortunately for me—or for the company, depending on how you want to look at it—that statement did not work out well. The next day I gathered my team and shared that I would be submitting my two weeks' notice. I didn't tell them why specifically. Look, I had stayed with the company because it had allowed me to lead in a way that agreed with my principles and values. There have been other offers made by other companies. I knew I wouldn't have an issue finding gainful employment. After that meeting I turned in my notice to resign to my supervisor. He instantly told me that I didn't have to do that, that something could be worked out. My response to him was that it was time for me to try something different. At this point he offered a pay increase and some other perks, but I knew within myself that this relationship was not going to work. He wanted me to lead in a way that wasn't a part of my leadership fabric. I did move on. You never know what lies ahead. I think the new supervisor and the unreasonable expectation was a test for me. I needed to get out of my comfort zone and consider other opportunities. I also needed to prove to myself that I would not compromise my leadership values for the sake of money. I want to reiterate here: I used the word "compromise," not "change." I stated earlier that maybe you may need to adjust the leadership style but not alter who you are as a leader. I got a better job that allowed me to be true to my principles and offered greater compensation. I maintained contact with some of the team. Within eighteen months Mike, Amber, and Jasmine had all moved on from the company.

Toolbox Alert: Take the time to write down your principles, qualities, and characteristics that you believe in your heart represent who you are. I know it sounds elementary, but trust me: in this world of aspirations and the desire to succeed, it's good to have a visible reference of who you are and who you want to be. This is extremely beneficial when you are placed in a position where you must decide whether you will compromise or hold firm to your character. True integrity is what you do when no one is around and how that action compares to who you say you are. Don't look in the mirror one day and not recognize who is staring back at you. The people who we lead trust us. Somewhere along the way, we showed them that we care. As a result of our caring, we were able to establish connections, and those connections garnered their commitment. Leadership true is a crossroads where you can continue to be true to who you are, or you can deviate and become something someone else wants you to be. If that something is contrary to the essence of who you are, then I encourage you to count the cost. It is my hope that once you count the cost, you will determine the cost is too great.

The Leadership Stride reminds leaders that all leaders don't lead the same way and with the same level of authenticity. Once you begin to sacrifice who you are as a leader, you can easily forget the type of leader that you truly are.

SUMMARY

To those of you who will read this book, I am hopeful that it will have an impact on your leadership ability. These are my experiences. Experiences that taught me so much about the awesome responsibility of leadership. The implications of leadership are much more than I envisioned them to be when I began my leadership path. I am convinced that the principles in The Leadership Stride will be a blessing to you and those you lead. Our families need and deserve more effective leadership. Our organizations, our churches and our communities are suffering with ineffective leadership or no leadership at all. Of course, this book is not a "cure all". It does however offer fresh perspective on the value of leadership and presents some strategies and principles to challenge us to do better and be better. From the very first chapter, Leadership Cred to the last chapter, Leadership True you will walk with me as I willingly embarked on the leadership journey.

I believe once a leader, always a leader. The only question is, "what type of leader will we be?" We all lead someone! Be credible and use your influence to help someone else along the way. Develop metrics that will enable the entire team to win. Capitalize on the reverberation of effective vision on those within the organization and those beyond. Be a thoughtful leader. Never underestimate the value of timely concise communication. Strive to have a culture that you and those you lead can be proud of. Don't be swayed by opportunities for elevation that require you to lead in a manner that conflicts with your character. That is the Leadership Stride.

I set out to write a book that would not be lengthy yet rewarding. When a person reads, they allow the author entry into their hearts and mind. Thank you for granting me access!

AFTERWORD

In this compelling memoir on leadership, the author shares a poignant journey, marked by personal trials and triumphs, offering readers an intimate look into his path to leadership. The narrative is not merely a recounting of personal growth; it serves as a guide for readers seeking to take a decisive step forward and gain their own "leadership stride". As each chapter unfolds a new facet of actionable steps, which when executed properly, open the door to achieving "sustainable leadership." The "Toolbox Alert" at the end of each chapter provides a short, but effective, knowledge nugget that can be swiftly put into practice.

....

Acacia D. Pereschuk

Senior Management and Program Analyst,
Federal Government

Captain
US Army, Retired

Milton Keynes UK
Ingram Content Group UK Ltd.
UKHW042226180324
439698UK00005B/512